ALL YOU NEED TO KNOW ABOUT BECOMING

How to be a Pop Star

Written

Contents

WANTED
Pop stars of the future!

Calling all singers, rappers, musicians and dancers! We're looking for talented young people to be the pop stars of the future. Step forward if you think this could be you!

Just imagine it – people all over the world could be listening to your music. You could have money and fame. You could travel and be on the covers of magazines. What's more, you could be doing what you love – making music.

If you think you have the voice, talent and style it takes to be a star ...

APPLY NOW!

Pop star checklist

Being a pop star isn't easy. If it were, everyone would do it!

To be a pop star you need …

	✔	✘
to have talent	✔	
to practise a lot	✔	
to learn the words for many songs	✔	
to perform concerts night after night	✔	
to travel long distances and work long hours	✔	
to be dedicated – and never give up.	✔	

Above all else, you need to love what you do!

Becoming a star

It can take a long time to become a star because there's so much to do and learn. This book tells you about some of those steps as well as giving you a chance to try things yourself. At the end you can take a quiz to find out if – just maybe – you've got what it takes to become a pop star one day.

Getting started

Starting young

Being a pop star is not as easy as you might think – in fact, it's actually a lot of hard work. Most pop stars start young. They work hard to develop the skills that will make them famous one day.

There's more to becoming a pop star than singing to yourself.

Say what?

" Obviously you never know what is going to happen. Singing is my dream but I need something to fall back on. I'm going to take my exams seriously. "

Nathan of The Wanted

Just in case

The music business is very competitive. Most pop stars work hard to finish school or college in case they don't fulfil their dreams. That's a lot of effort!

Learn to play

Pop stars don't just wake up one morning and discover they can sing or play the piano! They work at it. They take singing lessons and learn to play at least one musical instrument.

Many pop stars learn to play an instrument when they are young.

Justin Bieber only came second in his first singing competition – but it got him noticed!

Name: Justin Bieber
First single: *One Time*
Released: 2009

Justin loved music from an early age. He was four when he taught himself to play the drums. But that was only the start! At eight, he started to learn the guitar and then the keyboard and the trumpet. It wasn't until he was ten that he thought about singing!

Try it!

If you can't play an instrument, why not start now? Are there any classes you can attend? Can a friend teach you to play an instrument?

Practice makes perfect

Rehearsal time

To make it as a pop star takes a lot of practice. Even when stars are famous, they still spend hours rehearsing.

Practice Diary
My path to stardom!

Monday
Singing in the shower (does that count?)
Guitar practice after school (1 hr 30)

Tuesday
Guitar lesson (1 hr)
Practise guitar again after school (1 hr)

Wednesday
More singing in the shower (Mum wasn't happy!)
Singing lesson (1 hr)

Thursday
School choir (1 hr)
Band practice after school (2 hrs — voice tired!)

Top Tip
It helps to have a regular daily routine. Try practising before or after school every day.

Experts say that to succeed you have to practise for three hours a day for about ten years.

To avoid upsetting the neighbours, practise during the daytime or shut the windows to muffle the sound.

In the spotlight

It takes courage to perform in front of thousands of people. Pop stars might seem super-confident, but many of them admit they feel scared before a show. Having experience of being on stage when they were young helps a lot of pop stars overcome their nerves.

Choirs provide great opportunities to develop more confidence.

Taking part in performances regularly will help you build up confidence.

Top Tip

Build up confidence now by spending time in front of an audience. Volunteer to speak in assemblies, dance in shows or join a drama club.

Try it!

Put on a show for family and friends. Did they like it? Ask them to be honest – criticism is useful.

Building a band

The parts of a band

Imagine listening to a singer without a band. It wouldn't be the same without an accompaniment! There are no rules about what makes a perfect pop band. Different pop bands use different types of instrument, but these are the most popular.

The lead singer sings the main part of the song.

The lead guitarist plays the tune.

The drummer creates the main rhythm.

The bass guitarist plays the background **rhythms** and **chords**.

A band is like a jigsaw puzzle – when you put all the right pieces together it works perfectly!

Getting together

Pop bands form in lots of different ways. Some groups are made up of musicians who are friends. Some singers advertise for musicians to become their backing band and sometimes a **music manager** discovers people and puts a band together.

Put up adverts to find band members.

Be the One

So do you think you're the next BIG thing? We do!

We're called Going Places and we need a lead singer.

Join us and make all our dreams come true!
Call Simon on 077985431

Top Tip

To get valuable new members, make your advert really persuasive.

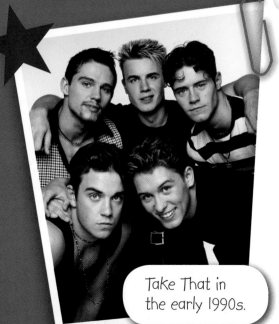

Take That in the early 1990s.

Name: Take That
Band formed: 1990
First single: Do What U Like

Before 1990, most of Take That didn't even know each other. Each member responded to an advert to be in the UK's next boy band. Within five years they were the biggest selling pop group in the UK since the Beatles!

Getting along

Staying together

One of the hardest challenges a band faces is staying together. Bands have a lot of decisions to make which can cause arguments. They have to work as a team and make joint decisions.

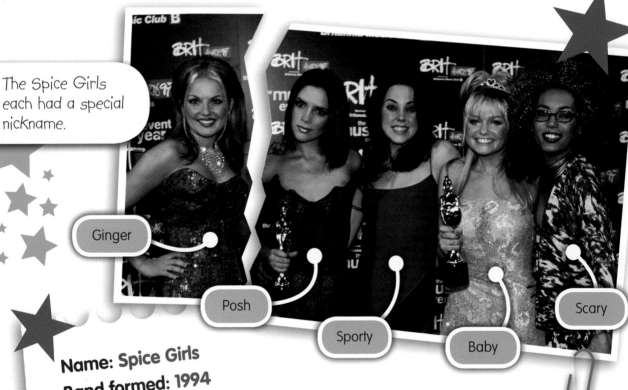

The Spice Girls each had a special nickname.

Ginger

Posh

Sporty

Baby

Scary

Name: Spice Girls
Band formed: 1994
First single: *Wannabe*

The Spice Girls were megastars! Their first single went to number one in 30 countries. They sold 75 million records worldwide and even starred in their own movie *Spiceworld*! Then in 2000 they disbanded. Some say this was because Geri ('Ginger') and the others fell out, but no one knows for sure!

What's in a name?

Pop stars don't always use their real names. They often use a made-up name called a stage name. Thinking of a new and unusual name isn't as easy as it sounds.

Choosing a name

Pop stars choose names in some strange ways! You probably don't know who Stefani Joanne Germanotta is, but I'm sure you've heard of Lady Gaga! So how did Stefani choose her name? Well, she was inspired by a song she loved – *Radio GaGa* by Queen.

STEVEN SPIELBERG Presents

MICHAEL J.

BACK TO THE FUTURE

A ROBERT ZEMECKIS Film

He was never in time for his classes...

He wasn't in time for his dinner....

Then one day... he wasn't in his time at all.

Marty McFly

Back to the Future was extremely popular in the 1980s. It tells the story of how Marty McFly goes back in time.

McFly don't have stage names but their band name is unusual. They're named after the lead singer's favourite character from the film *Back to the Future*.

Try it!

You may not be famous yet, but that shouldn't stop you. Try to think of your perfect stage name or even band name!

Making music

Musical genres

Every band or singer has their own sound, but they tend to fit into a particular musical genre. Pop, rock and rap are three of the most popular styles.

Pop

Pop is the style of music that is the most popular at any time. It usually consists of love songs with simple rhythms and **harmonies**.

Like many pop stars, Cheryl Cole records music you can dance to.

Kings of Leon is an American rock band that formed in 1999.

Rock

Rock is a type of music that has a strong beat. Most rock bands have an electric guitar, a bass guitar, drums and a singer.

Rap

In rap, words are spoken not sung. The **backing music** has a fast, strong rhythm.

Rappers like Dizzee Rascal often rap about problems young people face.

Copying your heroes

Copying isn't cheating when you're finding a musical style! Lots of pop stars admit they mimicked their music heroes when they were young. Listening to different styles of music has helped a lot of stars find their own sound.

Name: Taio Cruz
First single: *I Just Wanna Know*
Released: November 2006

When Taio Cruz was young he pretended to be his music heroes. He played tunes on the school piano and dreamed about performing with his idols. At the age of 18 he was signed to an American music label and was soon working with big names like Timbaland.

Taio Cruz had his first US and UK number one with the single *Break Your Heart*.

Try it!

Ask family and friends to share their favourite music with you. You might find a new musical style you like!

Writing songs

How it happens

Singing **covers** is fine when you start out, but to find true fame, pop stars really need their own songs. Writing pop songs can be difficult – you need to have original ideas for the words and for the music. That is why some pop stars pay songwriters and **composers** to create their songs. Others prefer to compose their own.

Name: Tom Fletcher
Band: McFly
First single: *Five Colours in Her Hair*
Released: 2004

McFly's lead singer Tom Fletcher first auditioned for Busted, but was asked to write songs for the band instead. He says it was former Busted star James Bourne who taught him how to put a good pop song together.

Tom Fletcher has written ten number one singles.

Taylor Swift performing at the Grammy Awards in 2010.

No Way!

You don't have to study composition to write songs. Taylor Swift wrote her first song, *Lucky You*, after learning just three guitar chords!

Inspiration

Songwriters find **inspiration** for songs in unusual places. They can get ideas from a newspaper headline or something they hear on a bus! Many songwriters are inspired by things that happen to them, or emotions they feel.

Jay-Z's hit song *Empire State of Mind* (sung with Alicia Keys) is a celebration of New York, where he grew up.

New York

Jay-Z

Alicia Keys

Try it!

Be inspired! Carry a notebook with you so that you can jot down memorable words or phrases you hear. You never know – these could be the start of your very first song!

Song lyrics

How songs work

Even songs have to follow rules – well, most of the time!
Pop songs often follow a similar pattern.

I miss you ...

> Pop song titles are usually simple like this.

I miss you every morning.
I miss you every night.
I miss you when I'm feeling down,
Even when I feel alright...

> This is the first **verse**. It tells us that the song is about missing somebody.

Please come back. Please come back.
Please don't stay away.
Please come back. Please come back.
Please don't stay away.

> The **chorus** is the part of a song that is sung after each verse.

I see your face on every one I meet.
I hear your laughter on every street.
I call your name but you're never there.
I try to understand, but it's just not fair...

> Notice how some of the lines rhyme.

> The second verse tells us more about the person's feelings.

Please come back. Please come back.
Please don't stay away.
Please come back. Please come back.
Please don't stay away.

> This is a repeat of the chorus. A catchy chorus stays in your head!

How to write a song

There are six steps many artists follow when writing a song.

1. Find a good title for your new song.

2. Create a simple but catchy tune.

3. Use the first verse to tell listeners what the theme of the song is.

4. Repeat a catchy phrase in the chorus.

5. Use the other verses to tell more of the story.

6. Finish with a chorus, or a final verse to end the story.

Try to write a song with patterns just like a poem!

Try it!

Find a line from something that inspires you. Write down ideas for how this could become a song.

Get the look

Creating an image

Singing great songs isn't enough to make you a pop idol. You need a great image too. Pop stars spend a long time choosing a look. They also use **stylists** to make sure they stand out from the crowd and look fantastic.

Lady Gaga changes her outfits up to ten times in every show. That's a lot of new clothes!

Stage style

So what makes the perfect look? Some stage outfits are so wacky that stars have to check they can move in them before going on stage! Pop stars often experiment with lots of different styles and change their outfits several times.

Say what?

" Fashion is everything. When I'm writing music, I'm thinking about the clothes I want to wear on stage. "

Lady Gaga

Superstar styles

A pop star's look has to be eye-catching, and it also needs to match their music. Think of a superstar and you should immediately be able to imagine the type of music they play.

The Kings of Leon have their own fashion range.

Pop stars	Key look	Type of music
Black Eyed Peas	Mixture of styles – layers of clothes, hats and sunglasses	Rap
Cheryl Cole	High fashion	Pop
Kings of Leon	Skinny jeans, check shirts and boots	Rock

People try to copy Cheryl Cole's look.

The Black Eyed Peas' look changes to match the changing style of their music.

Try it!

Try to copy your favourite pop star's latest look or create a look of your own. It doesn't have to cost a lot. Can you make your old clothes into a new outfit? Remember: consult your mum or dad about this!

Dance to the music

Into the groove

An important part of a pop star's performance is moving on stage. Pop stars who dance to their music are exciting to watch – they make you want to dance to their music too! But not all pop stars know how to dance. Some have to work hard to learn dance moves and improve their performance.

Lots of people copy JLS's dance routines.

Say what?

❝ I love to dance but you know, we're not exactly trained dancers in any sort of way ... It's more enjoyable to perform when you've got a slick little move though. ❞

Aston from JLS

Dance moves

There are many different dance steps pop stars have to learn.
This one is good for dancing to rap music.

1. Start with your right leg in the air.

2. Lean forward and hop on your left foot.
   It should look like a backwards skip!

3. Shift your weight backwards onto your
   right foot. Your left leg should now be in
   the air and your right foot on the ground.

4. Now repeat each step until you can do
   it quickly and smoothly.

A good way to learn new moves
is to join a dance class.

Try it!

Try doing the dance step on this page.
Can you think of some moves of your
own? Now try doing the steps to music.

On stage

Stage fright

Once a pop star has a song, an outfit and dance moves – what's left to do? It's time to get on stage.

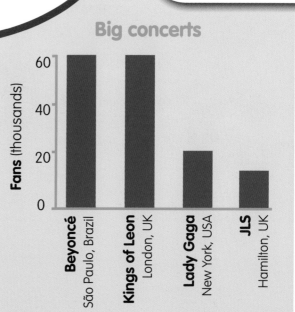

Miley Cyrus grew confident about stage performances when she had the lead role in the hit US TV show *Hannah Montana*.

Say what?

" Places that I'm not familiar with I do get a bit nervous, but when I get out there, I forget all about it. "

Miley Cyrus talks about going on stage.

Sometimes pop stars perform in front of thousands of fans.

Stay cool

To keep cool before a show some pop stars watch TV, read a book or exercise. For some people, fear is a good thing – it helps them to perform their best – and sometimes pop stars just learn to deal with it.

Big concerts

Fans (thousands)

60

40

20

0

Beyoncé São Paulo, Brazil

Kings of Leon London, UK

Lady Gaga New York, USA

JLS Hamilton, UK

Being great on stage

Many people are talented singers and dancers, but to become a star you need a great stage act too. Some stars use **props** like smoke-machines or flashing lights. The best pop stars make every song a memorable performance.

No Way!

Props can help to make a stage show exciting, but take care. In 2010 Pink slipped out of a harness that was lifting her over the audience.

Luckily Pink wasn't badly hurt when she fell!

Try it!

To relax before you perform, try deep breathing for five minutes! Close your eyes and breathe in and out, very slowly and very deeply. It works!

Finding fame

Getting noticed

The work isn't over yet! To find fame, pop stars need to get noticed. No one is going to buy their albums if they haven't heard of them! So how do pop stars find fame?

Name: Lily Allen
First single: *Smile*
Released: 2006

In 2005 Lily Allen composed and sang songs, but she wasn't a star. Few people had heard of her. So she started to post her songs on the Internet. Tens of thousands of people logged on to watch and listen to her, and a year later she got her first **record contract**.

In 2010 Lily Allen won the **Brit Award** for British Female Solo Artist of the Year.

Non-stop work

Wannabe pop stars have to work hard – they tour the country doing shows and music festivals. They play anywhere they can, often without being paid. They put some of their songs online. They do all they can to make sure as many people as possible hear about them.

Power to the fans

Without fans, there is no fame. **Publicity** gets pop stars attention and fans.

Pop videos are great for publicity. They can help people get noticed and remembered.

Talent shows

Another way pop stars get noticed is by participating in TV singing competitions. Performing on TV each week gives them the chance to win fans as well as votes.

Top Tip

Make sure every show is the best it can be. If people like you, they'll tell their friends about you.

Girls Aloud found fame after winning a TV talent show in 2002.

Being famous

A busy life

Being famous looks like great fun. After all, you get to travel the world, wear great clothes and do what you love. But pop stars are often too busy rehearsing, recording and touring to relax and enjoy themselves!

> " I don't think that you can prepare for fame or get used to it. "
>
> Lady Gaga

When you're famous, it's hard to organise a quiet day off. Fans and photographers follow you everywhere!

Monday 7th January

8 a.m.	Radio interview
10 a.m.	Gym
11 a.m.	Hairdresser
12 – 3 p.m.	Rehearsals on stage
4 p.m.	Newspaper interview
7 p.m.– midnight	Concert!

Tuesday 8th January

7 a.m.	Interview on Breakfast TV
9 a.m.	Rehearse for pop video
4.30 p.m.	Magazine photo shoot
7 p.m.– midnight	Concert!

Pop stars have a full timetable!

Talk about it

Fans like to get to know their pop idols. That's why pop stars have to do lots of interviews. Fans don't just want to hear about a star's music – they also want to know how they became noticed, what pets they have and who their best friend is!

LL Cool J interviews the Jonas Brothers during the Grammy Nominations Concert.

Be prepared

Interviewers sometimes ask pop stars strange or tricky questions. How would you answer questions like these if you were famous?

If you were an animal, what would you be?

What's your worst habit?

What's the worst thing about being famous?

What did you dream about last night?

Who is the most annoying band member?

Try it!

Be prepared! Practise for the future: take turns with your friends to be a pop star and an interviewer. Ask and find good answers for some tricky questions.

Staying famous

Keeping fans happy

Once pop stars are famous, they can relax, can't they? No, not really. They have to keep their fans happy, and to do that they have to keep releasing great new music and producing great new shows!

Top Tip

Being famous can be tough. Some people will be unkind about your appearance and won't like your music. Most stars cope with this by ignoring negative comments and believing in themselves. This is hard to do, though!

Keep at it

To stay famous, pop stars keep up the hard work. They experiment with new looks. They exercise and eat lots of fruit and vegetables to stay healthy. They listen to other people's music to get new ideas for their own songs and they learn new dance routines.

Will pop fans be screaming for you like this one day?

Real pop idols!

These artists have sold millions of albums since their first singles were released.

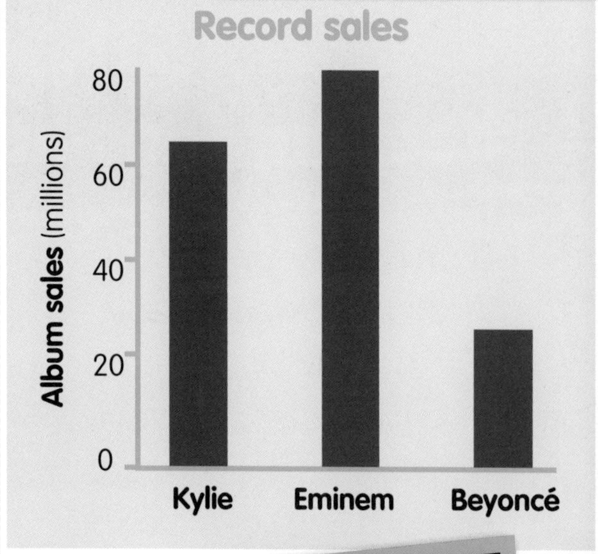

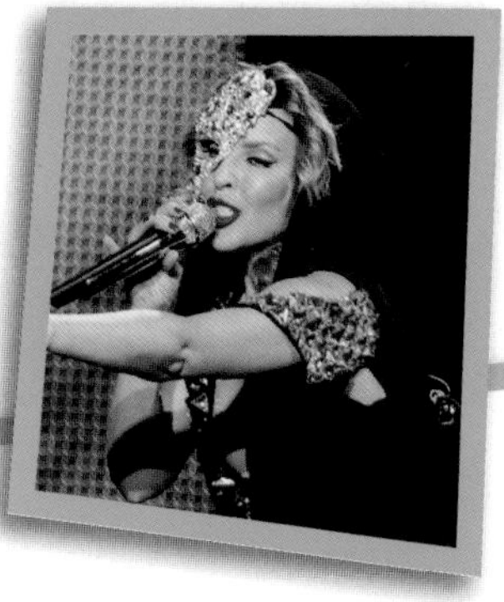

Kylie

Kylie has never stopped working hard to improve. She's always trying to make her shows, style and music better and better.

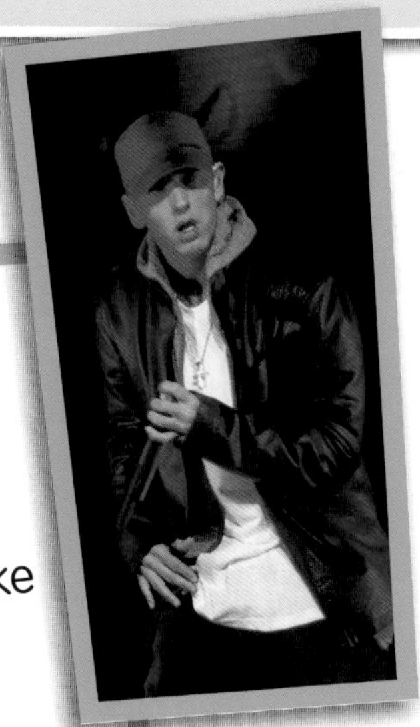

Eminem

Eminem is the biggest-selling rap artist in the world. His daring pop videos and stories about his private life keep him in the news, and fans like his clever, sometimes funny and honest **lyrics**.

Beyoncé

Beyoncé won a school talent contest at six, and has never looked back! She works non-stop but always smiles and is polite when interviewed.

Have you got what it takes?

Do you think you have what it takes to become the next pop idol? Take the quiz and find out!

1

You want to be a pop star one day. How do you get started?

A   Start practising now for at least two hours a day.

B   Practise at least three times a week.

C   Relax! You don't need to practise. You're brilliant already!

2

You're the lead singer in a band. How do you plan your next move?

A   Make all decisions as a group.

B   Discuss things but make the final decision yourself.

C   Make all the decisions yourself. You know what the right answer is!

3 You're trying to find your music style. How do you do it?

A Listen to lots of different types of music. You never know what will inspire you.

B Listen to your favourite music over and over again.

C Listen only to your own songs.

4 How do you go about performing your songs?

A Ensure every song is performed brilliantly.

B Ensure you perform your favourite songs really well.

C Avoid working on the stage act because the songs speak for themselves.

5 You've made it. How do you act now you're a world famous star?

A Keep working hard, finding ways to improve your style and music.

B Work hard but keep your music the same because that's how people like it.

C Take it easy because you are already famous.

How did you do?

Mostly As
Congratulations. You've got star quality. I can almost hear screaming fans outside your house now!

Mostly Bs
Well done. You've made a great start. Keep it up.

Mostly Cs
Oh dear, you have a lot to learn. Being a pop star requires really hard work. Maybe you should reread the book!

Glossary

backing music music that accompanies the singer or tune

Brit Award British music award

chord group of notes played together

chorus set of lines in a song, which is repeated two or more times

composer someone who writes music

cover version of someone else's song

harmonies notes that are played together to make a pleasing sound

inspiration something that gives someone ideas to be creative

lyrics words to a song

music manager person who sorts out the business side of a band

props objects used in a show

publicity attention from newspapers, TV and other media

record contract legal agreement between a band and a record company to make records

rhythm repeated pattern of sounds

stylist person who helps others create an image or style

verse group of lines in a poem or song

Index